TECHNOLOGY COLLECTION TRENDS

in the
U.S. Defense Industry

2 0 0 6

DEFENSE SECURITY SERVICE
1340 BRADDOCK PLACE
ALEXANDRIA, VA 22314-1651

The Defense Security Service (DSS) is responsible for assisting the U.S. cleared defense industry in identifying and reporting foreign contacts and collection attempts, as outlined in the National Industrial Security Program Operating Manual (NISPOM). The DSS annual publication, Technology Collection Trends in U.S. Defense Industry, has its foundations in the Suspicious Contact Reports received from the cleared defense industry.

This publication identifies foreign collection trends directed at U.S. defense industry so that U.S. technologies and classified information may be better protected. The research, analyses, and assessments in this document are directed to security officials, cleared defense contractors, intelligence professionals, and Department of Defense policymakers and decisionmakers. This document identifies the most frequently targeted U.S. technologies, the preferred collection methods, entities attempting the collection, and the regions where collection originates.

Our goal is to provide the defense industrial community with technology collection trends to enhance threat awareness and to protect U.S. technology from foreign entities. In order to accomplish this goal, cleared defense contractors are charged with submitting certain reports in accordance with the NISPOM. DSS strongly encourages all Facility Security Officers to conduct Security Education, Training and Awareness (SETA) at their facilities. Increased SETA results in more reporting and identification of threats both within and beyond the industrial base. Timely submission of Suspicious Contact Reports to DSS field offices is critical to an effective Industrial Security Program.

This document would not be possible without the strong support of Facility Security Officers within the U.S. cleared defense industry. DSS thanks the U.S. cleared defense industry for their continued support of the NISPOM and its contributions to this annual publication.

KATHLEEN M. WATSON
Acting Director

Contents

Front cover photo courtesy of Sandia National Laboratories, SUMMiT^{TM} Technologies. All other photos courtesy of the Department of Defense.

The *2006 Technology Collection Trends in the U.S. Defense Industry* was prepared by the Defense Security Service Counterintelligence (DSSCI) Office. Direct comments/questions, feedback, or requests for additional copies to OCI@DSS.SMIL.MIL or by mail to DSSCI, 1340 Braddock Place, Alexandria, VA 22314. This document is also posted at WWW.DSS.SMIL.MIL.

I. Introduction

The Defense Security Service (DSS) Counterintelligence (CI) Office presents the 10th annual Technology Collection Trends in the U.S. Defense Industry - 2006 as a tool for security professionals. The technology collection trends and assessments in this publication are based upon suspicious contact reports originating from cleared defense industry. These contact reports describe suspicious foreign activity targeting U.S. personnel, technologies, classified information, and export controlled products throughout the cleared defense industry.

Foreign entities target the U.S. cleared defense industry because our organizations research, develop, and manufacture advanced dual-use (commercial and military) technologies and products. Consequently, the U.S. defense industry is the most important player when it comes to safeguarding information critical to our national security. The National Industrial Security Program (NISP) exists to ensure the cleared defense industry protects classified information while performing work on bids, contracts, programs, and research and development projects. Though the NISP is an effective program for mitigating the loss of classified technology and information, it is essential that all cleared defense industry leaders, supervisors, and employees recognize the foreign collection threat. An effective security education and training program can enhance employees' knowledge of the foreign collection threat to the U.S. defense industry. Properly trained, security conscious employees are our best defense against foreign collection.

This publication identifies technology collection trends, general information, and conclusions to assist cleared defense industry personnel with identifying and reporting suspicious foreign activity. The research in this document also provides the cleared defense industry a tool to implement responsive, threat specific, and cost-effective security countermeasures. Government agencies are encouraged to use this annual publication to evaluate specific threats and develop additional security countermeasures.

Please note that percentages throughout this document may not total to exactly 100 percent due to rounding. All information is based on Fiscal Year 2005 reports from cleared defense industry.

II. Executive Summary

A. Reporting Trends

This report is based on an analysis of 971 Suspicious Contact Reports (SCR) received in Fiscal Year 2005 from cleared defense contractors, DSS Industrial Security Representatives (ISR) and Field Counterintelligence Specialists (FCIS). The total number of SCR in 2005 increased by almost 43 percent. This significant increase may reflect greater threat awareness among employees at cleared facilities. In 2005, 342 cleared defense contractors, or 3 percent of the U.S. cleared defense industry, reported suspicious foreign contacts to DSS.

B. Country Trends

In 2005, DSS identified 106 countries associated with suspicious activities based on U.S. cleared defense industry reporting, up from 90 countries in 2004. However, aside from a few countries that appear in SCR each year, the identified countries do not remain stable. Some new countries appear; others drop out. The top ten collecting countries in 2005 accounted for 79.9 percent of all suspicious activity. Of these, the top five collecting countries represented 57.4 percent of all such activity.

C. Technology Interests Trends

Information Systems Technology, due to its potential for enhancing the efficiency of command, control, communications, and intelligence will continue as a priority technology target for many countries. The steady increase in incidents over the past two years where foreign entities have targeted modeling and simulation technology is also noteworthy. It may be a reflection of the growing number of weapons develop-ment programs in many countries as they attempt to emulate U.S. technological advances.

Suspicious Internet Activity against cleared defense contractors also increased this year. The potential gain from even one successful computer intrusion makes it an attractive, relatively low-risk, option for any country seeking access to sensitive information stored on U.S. computer networks. The risk to sensitive information on U.S. computer systems will increase as more countries develop capabilities to exploit those systems.

D. Most Frequently Reported Technology Targets

The following technologies generated the most foreign interest in 2005:

- -- Information Systems - 21.8%
- -- Lasers & Optics - 10.7%
- -- Aeronautics - 9.7%
- -- Sensors - 9.5%
- -- Armaments & Energetic Materials - 9.2%
- -- Electronics - 6.6%
- -- Space Systems - 6.5%
- -- Marine Systems - 4.8%
- -- Materials & Processing - 4%
- -- Signature Control - 3.6%

The top ten targeted technologies identified above accounted for 86.2 percent. Overall, a comparison of 2004 and 2005's top ten targeted technologies revealed minimal changes. The most targeted technology remained Information Systems with 21.8 percent of all SCRs.

E. Most Frequently Reported Foreign Collection Methods of Operation (MO)

MO are the techniques or tradecraft used to collect intelligence or information from cleared defense contractors. In 2005, the most frequently used MO were:

-- Requests for Information - 34.2%
-- Acquisition of Controlled Technology
-- 32.2%
-- Solicitation of Marketing Services - 9.6%
-- Exploitation of Relationships - 5.3%
-- Suspicious Internet Activity - 5.3%
-- Exploitation of a Foreign Visit (CONUS) - 4.6%
-- Other - 3.1%
-- Targeting at Conventions, Expositions, or Seminars - 4.3%
-- Cultural Commonality - 0.9%
-- Foreign Employees - 0.6%

The top three MO totaled 76 percent of all foreign collection attempts reported to DSS. In 2005, there were fewer reported suspicious contacts involving Requests for Information (RFI) than last year and a marked increase in Acquisition of Controlled Technology. In 2004, RFI accounted for 47.5 percent of reported MOs, and Acquisition of Controlled Technology represented 20 percent. This year, Acquisition of Controlled Technology has nearly equaled RFI as the most preferred technique for targeting cleared defense contractors.

For a complete listing of foreign collection MOs and their definitions, please see Section VII, Appendix 1, on pages 22-27.

III. World Collection Trends

Table 1: World Collection Trends 1997-2005

Year	1997	1998	1999	2000	2001	2002	2003	2004	2005
Number of Countries with Identified Collection Involvement	37	47	56	63	75	84	85	90	106

A. Worldwide Breakdown by Region. In 2005, DSS identified 106 countries associated with suspicious collection activities. This was an increase of 16 targeting countries as compared to 2004 data. However, there were 15 countries with reported collection attempts in 2004 that did not garner a suspicious contact report in 2005. In addition, there were 30 countries identified with suspicious contact reporting in 2005 that did not appear in 2004 data. While many of these countries are as technologically advanced as the United States, others are developing or underdeveloped countries who attempt to acquire information and technologies for diversion to more technologically advanced nations.

The regions in Figure 1 are organized by the U.S. Department of State's six regional groupings. These groupings represent areas of the world that share political, religious, and cultural similarities among countries in those parts of the world. In 2005, the majority of reported targeting originated from East Asia and the Pacific, which accounted for 31 percent of all reporting. The Near East made up 23.1 percent of the targeting, Eurasia had 19.3 percent of the targeting, and South Asia had 13.2 percent. Finally, Africa and the Western Hemisphere (minus U.S.) accounted for a minority of targeting with a combined total of 11.5 percent of the reports.

B. Foreign Collectors. DSS identifies types of collectors after evaluating reported information, conducting extensive research, and assessing relationships and representatives in each incident. Each collection

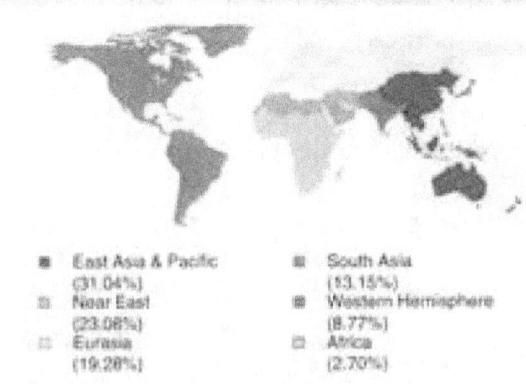

East Asia & Pacific (31.04%)
Near East (23.08%)
Eurasia (19.28%)
South Asia (13.15%)
Western Hemisphere (8.77%)
Africa (2.70%)

Figure 1: The map above reflects the regions where collection efforts originated or the anticipated end user of the targeted technology. The associated percentages indicate the level of collection reported in 2005. The map does not imply national-level support of the collection activity. Collectors may have based their operation in a third country to conceal intentions or identity of the ultimate end-user of collected technology.

attempt is categorized as originating from a government entity, government affiliated entity, commercial firm, individual, or unknown entity.

Foreign government sponsored targeting, which includes Ministry of Defense, Intelligence Officers (including foreign military attaches), and other official government entities accounted for 22.8 percent of all reported cases in 2005. This represented a slight increase from 2004 for "traditional" (direct foreign government) targeting.

Government affiliated entities include research institutes, laboratories, government-funded universities, contractors representing governments, and foreign companies whose work is exclusively or predominantly in support of foreign government agencies. Reported targeting by government affiliated collectors experienced a marked increase from 2004. Government affiliated entities had accounted for 15.3 percent of all targeting, but in 2005 they accounted for 28.9 percent of targeting.

Collection attempts by foreign commercial activities indicated a slight decline in targeting during 2005. Foreign commercial activities are those companies engaged in business, whether in the commercial or defense sectors, whose suspicious activity is not identified with a foreign government. Many of these commercial collectors may be acting in response to foreign government issued requests for products and technology that will be incorporated into indigenous weapons systems.

Targeting by individual foreign collectors decreased slightly in 2005, marking a second year of declines. Foreign individuals include those persons for whom DSS has

been unable to identify an affiliation due to a lack of information, such as where only a name or e-mail address is known. It is clear that the majority of these incidents involved foreign sponsorship or affiliation. A small percentage in the data was identified as people seeking personal financial gain.

At least 13 percent of targeting was conducted by entities with no known affiliation. This group of collection attempts often did not indicate the name of the requester, an email address, or any other identifying information.

C. Methods of Operation. DSS analyzes each collection attempt to determine the method of operation (MO) employed by a collector, which allows for a better understanding of the tools and techniques used to target the U.S. defense industry. The most common MO is a direct request for information. These events are associated with email, phone, and mail correspondence directed to a facility and posing specific and detailed questions that would entail the release of sensitive or classified information if answered. In 2005, 34.2 percent of all reported collection attempts involved a request for information. This is a decrease from 2004 data, which could be attributable to an increase in attempted direct acquisitions as a means to collect technology. This year the use of Acquisition of Technology as a method increased, accounting for 32.2 percent of all reported cases. Often these incidents initially appear to be legitimate sales opportunities for contractors. However, as the transaction proceeds it may eventually involve the violation of export laws or an illegal diversion of the purchased technology to an unlawful end user. The third most popular MO in 2005 was Solicitation and Marketing of Services. It experienced a slight decrease and accounted for 9.6 percent of all collection attempts. While solicitation decreased, Exploitation of a Foreign Visit as an MO remained relatively stable between 2004 and 2005, accounting for about five percent of all targeting.

The remaining MO combined for less than 15 percent of collection attempts. Although these MO are not as broadly used as the previously mentioned methods, it does not mean that they are not as successful or do not pose as high a threat. Suspicious Internet Activity, for example, accounted for only five percent of the total targeting. However, the impact of a successful collection via this MO can be exponentially more damaging than that of other methods due to the potential for collecting massive amounts of information from just one computer intrusion event.

IV. TECHNOLOGY SECTION

DSS analyzes foreign interest in critical U.S. defense technology in terms of the 20 categories found in the Militarily Critical Technologies List (MCTL), Volume III. The Department of Defense assesses the technologies in Volume III as critical in maintaining superior U.S. military capabilities. Volume III serves as the template for DSS to define categories and subcategories for each technology.

Of the 971 incidents in 2005 that formed the basis for this publication, some involved multiple technologies. Therefore, the percentages derived from those cases are based on the number of attempts against MCTL categories and not on the total number of DSS cases.

A. INFORMATION SYSTEMS TECHNOLOGY

Table 2

FY05 Information Systems Technology Sub-Categories	
Sub-Category	Percent
Information Communications	16.90%
Information Exchange	1.15%
Information Processing	4.23%
Information Security	7.31%
Information Management and Control	3.85%
Information Systems and Facilities	3.08%
Information Sensing	0.38%
Information Visualization and Representation	3.85%
Modeling and Simulation	16.92%
Information Technology (Uncategorized)	42.31%

Overview

Again in 2005, Information Systems Technology was targeted at a rate almost twice that of any other technology category. This continues a trend seen since 2003. The most frequently targeted subcategories of Information Systems Technology were information communications, and modeling and simulation. Each of these subcategories accounted for 17 percent of incidents related to Information Systems Technology. The steady increase in incidents targeting modeling and simulation technology during 2004 and 2005 is noteworthy. This could reflect an upsurge in weapons development programs in the regions

indicating increased interest in this category: East Asia and Pacific, and the Near East.

Table 3

FY05 Information Systems Top Ten Methods of Operation		
Rank	Method of Operation	Percent
1	Request for Information	36.48%
2	Exploitation of a foreign visit (CONUS)	2.93%
3	Exploitation of Relationships	4.23%
4	Acquisition of Controlled Technology	23.45%
5	Suspicious Internet Activity	7.17%
6	Targeting at Conventions/Expositions/Seminars	7.82%
7	Solicitation of Marketing Services	14.01%
8	Cultural Commonality	1.30%
9	Other	2.61%

Perhaps the most notable change in the Information Systems Technology category this year is the shift in affiliation of the foreign collectors from commercial to government and government affiliated. Overall affiliations were more evenly spread among government, government affiliated, and commercial than last year.

Examples of the technologies sought include: Ka-band satellite communications systems, electronic warfare simulation systems, software-based simulation systems, tactical communication radios, SIGINT/COMINT equipment, and global positioning systems.

Image 1: Technician working on FLTSATCOM

MCTL Vol. III Technology Categories

Table 2 depicts the collection activity as reported by U.S. cleared defense contractors in 2005 for the Information Systems Technology category. For an explanation of the technologies covered by each subcategory, please refer to the MCTL, Volume III.

Collection Attempts by Region

Countries of the East Asia and Pacific region were again the most active collectors in this technology category during 2005, accounting for 34.6 percent of all reported attempts. This is an

---

Collection Activity by Region

- East Asia & Pacific (34.62%)
- Near East (29.29%)
- Eurasia (17.46%)
- South Asia (9.47%)
- Western Hemisphere (7.40%)
- Africa (1.78%)

---

eight percent increase over last year, and continues a trend of increases since 2003. Countries of the Near East accounted for 29.3 percent of attempts, a seven percent increase over last year. Africa and Eurasia indicated a decrease in collection attempts from last year, to 1.8 percent and 17.5 percent respectively.

Methods of Operation

On Table 3, Requests For Information (RFI) accounted for approximately 36.5 percent of incidents related to Information Systems Technology. This was the most frequently used MO. However, RFI in 2005 were significantly less than last year's 52.5 percent of incidents. Acquisitions of Controlled Technology indicated a significant increase this year, from 3.3 percent in 2004 to 23.5 percent. Additionally, increased incidents of Suspicious Internet Activity, from five to 7.2 percent, is cause for concern. A single compromise

of a cleared defense contractor's unclassified network could reveal details of multiple weapon systems in development.

B. LASERS AND OPTICS TECHNOLOGY

Overview

The Lasers and Optics category was the second most targeted technology this year, moving from sixth place in 2004. This technology category saw the greatest amount of change in regional interest: East Asia and Pacific moved from second place to first, with a 12 percent increase over last year.

Incidents involving government affiliated collectors increased as well. Finally, the most employed MO was Acquisition of Controlled Technology, with an increase of nine percent from last year.

Examples of technology in this category sought by foreign entities are: Night vision systems, eye-safe laser range finders, optical processing systems, light detection and ranging (LIDAR) systems, adaptive optics systems, stabilized optical sight systems, and focal plane arrays.

MCTL Vol. III Technology Categories

Table 4

FY05 Lasers & Optics Technology Sub-Categories

Sub-Category	Percent
Lasers	29.92%
Optics	24.41%
Optical Materials and Processes	4.72%
Supporting Technologies and Applications	5.51%
Optoelectronics and Photonics Technology	5.51%
Lasers and Optics (Uncategorized)	29.92%

Table 4 shows the collection activity as reported by cleared U.S. defense contractors in 2005 for the Lasers and Optics Technology category. For an explanation of the technologies covered by each subcategory, please refer to the MCTL, Volume III.

Collection Attempts by Region

Industry reports in 2005 indicated a strong foreign interest in Lasers and Optics Technology. This technology category saw the greatest change in regional interest. A significant increase in incidents involving the East Asia and Pacific region, from 22.7 percent to 35 percent, occurred

Collection Activity by Region

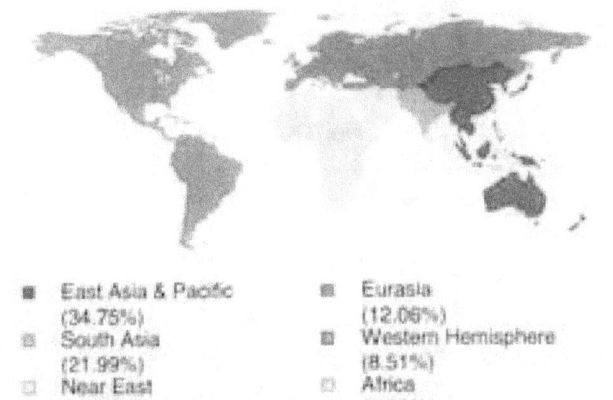

- East Asia & Pacific (34.75%)
- South Asia (21.99%)
- Near East (21.28%)
- Eurasia (12.06%)
- Western Hemisphere (8.51%)
- Africa (1.42%)

this year. South Asia indicated a slight increase, from 18.2 percent to 22 percent, which moved it to second place. Incidents involving the Near East decreased this year, from 26 percent to 21.3 percent, moving it into third place. Eurasia indicated a significant decrease in reported activity in this category, from 24.2 percent to 12.1 percent. Finally, the Western Hemisphere stayed roughly the same as last year, comprising 8.5 percent of incidents in this technology category.

Methods of Operation

Table 5 depicts Acquisition of Controlled Technology, with 38 percent of incidents, as the most frequently reported MO in 2005. It increased nine percent from 2004. RFI decreased from 45 percent of incidents to 37 percent this year. Finally, Suspicious Internet Activity increased from 2.9 percent to 4.4 percent of industry reports. Although commercial affiliation continued to be the largest identified segment at 33 percent, the percentage of government affiliated collectors increased from 19 percent last year to 29 percent in 2005.

Table 5

	FY05 Lasers & Optics Top Ten Methods of Operation	
Rank	Method of Operation	Percent
1	Request for Information	36.50%
2	Exploitation of a foreign visit (CONUS)	2.92%
3	Exploitation of Relationships	4.38%
4	Acquisition of Controlled Technology	37.96%
5	Suspicious Internet Activity	4.38%
6	Targeting at Conventions/Expositions/Seminars	1.46%
7	Solicitation of Marketing Services	8.03%
8	Foreign Employees	2.19%
9	Other	2.19%

C. AERONAUTICS TECHNOLOGY

Overview

Aeronautics Technology was the third most targeted technology in 2005, continuing a trend that began last year. East Asian and Pacific regional entities were most active in targeting this technology category.

Image 2: Soldier aims a DRAGON anti-tank system

One significant change in this category was the dramatic increase in incidents involving government affiliated entities. However, the most significant change was in MOs: Acquisition of Controlled Technology increased from 8.7 percent last year to 31 percent in 2005. RFI, however, continued to be the most employed MO.

Table 6

FY05 Aeronautics Technology Sub-Categories

Sub-Category	Percent
Aerodynamics	3.48%
Aeronautical Propulsion	13.04%
Aeronautical Structures	10.43%
Aeronautical Vehicle Control	2.61%
Aeronautical Subsystems and Components	17.39%
Aeronautical Design and Systems Integration	5.22%
Aeronautics (Uncategorized)	47.83%

Examples of technology sought are: Military-related aircraft engines, tactical unmanned aerial vehicles (UAV), avionics systems for UAV and fighter aircraft, missile launch warning systems, advanced engine technologies, maritime patrol aircraft avionics and systems, and ground test equipment.

MCTL Vol. III Technology Categories

Table 6 depicts the collection activity as reported by cleared U.S. defense contractors in 2005 for the Aeronautics Technology category. For an explanation of the technologies covered by each subcategory, please refer to the MCTL, Volume III.

Collection Activity by Region

- East Asia & Pacific (31.04%)
- Near East (23.08%)
- Eurasia (15.67%)
- South Asia (14.18%)
- Western Hemisphere (12.69%)
- Africa (0.00%)

Collection Attempts by Region

Entities from the East Asia and Pacific region were the most active in 2005 at 31 percent of industry reports in this technology category. Incidents involving the Near East increased from 18.1 percent last year to 23.1 percent in 2005. Eurasia indicated a decrease in incidents, from

Table 7

FY05 Aeronautics Top Ten Methods of Operation

Rank	Method of Operation	Percent
1	Request for Information	35.17%
2	Exploitation of a foreign visit (CONUS)	4.14%
3	Exploitation of Relationships	8.28%
4	Acquisition of Controlled Technology	31.03%
5	Suspicious Internet Activity	4.14%
6	Cultural Commonality	0.69%
7	Targeting at Conventions/Expositions/Seminars	3.45%
8	Solicitation of Marketing Services	9.66%
9	Foreign Employees	0.69%
10	Other	2.76%

28.2 percent in 2004 to 15.7 percent this year. Finally, South Asia and the Western Hemisphere showed minimal changes from last year.

Methods of Operation

On Table 7, reports of suspicious incidents from cleared defense contractors in 2005 indicate that the most used MO to target aeronautics technology was RFI. This MO was 35.2 percent of incidents in this category. Acquisition of Controlled Technology, at 31 percent, increased significantly from 8.7 percent last year. Government affiliated entities were identified in 30.6 percent of incidents, which is a significant increase over last year's 15.8 percent. Commercial entities accounted for 29.6 percent of targeting activity in this category.

D. SENSORS TECHNOLOGY

Overview

Industry reports of incidents in the Sensors Technology category decreased from 45.7 percent last year to 9.5 percent in 2005. This changed its relative position among targeted technology categories from second to fourth. Most incidents in this category involved East Asian and Pacific regional entities, with a 10 percent increase over last year.

RFI represented the primary MO to target Sensors Technology in 2005. However, a significant increase occurred in actual attempts to acquire the technology through various schemes to bypass restrictions imposed by the International Trafficking in Arms Regulation. Such incidents of Acquisition of Controlled Technology increased from 13.4 percent in 2004 to 26 per-

10

cent this year. Incidents that involved foreign governments remained stable, and commercial entities' activity indicated a decline.

Table 8

FY05 Sensors Technology Sub-Categories

Sub-Category	Percent
Acoustic Sensors, Terrestrial Platform	1.77%
Acoustic Sensors, Marine, Active Sonar	4.42%
Acoustic Sensors, Marine, Passive Sonar	4.42%
Acoustic Sensors, Marine Platform	2.65%
Electro-optic Sensors	12.39%
Radar	39.82%
Land Mine Countermeasures	0.88%
Sensors (Uncategorized)	33.63%

Examples of Sensors Technology sought include: Missile launch warning systems, 3D radar systems, electronic warfare systems, sonar systems, maritime surface search radars, geo-acoustic and seismic sensors, target tracking systems.

MCTL Vol. III Technology Categories

Table 8 shows the collection activity as reported by cleared U.S. defense contractors in 2005 for the Sensors Technology category. For an explanation of the technologies covered by each sub-category, please refer to the MCTL, Volume III.

Image 3: Radar operator at work

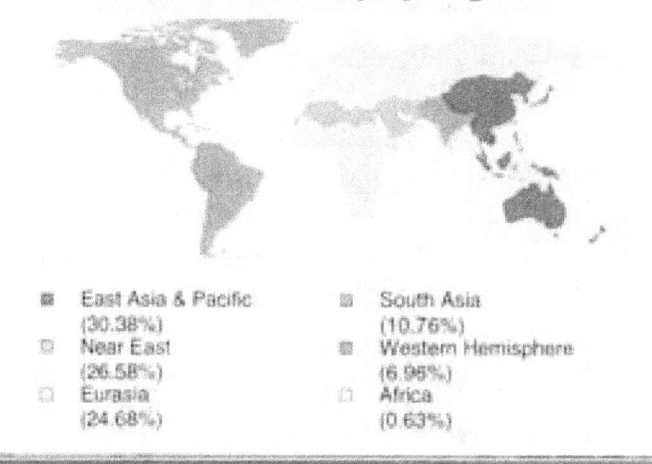

Collection Activity by Region

- ▣ East Asia & Pacific (30.38%)
- ▫ Near East (26.58%)
- ▫ Eurasia (24.68%)
- ▣ South Asia (10.76%)
- ▣ Western Hemisphere (6.96%)
- ▫ Africa (0.63%)

Collection Attempts by Region

East Asia and Pacific entities were the most active in targeting Sensors Technology in 2005. Incidents involving this region rose from 20 percent in 2004 to 30.4 percent this year. The Near East also indicated an increase over last year, to 26.6 percent. Incidents involving Eurasia accounted for 24.7 percent, or roughly the same level as in 2004. Africa, South Asia, and Western Hemisphere all indicated decreased activity.

Methods of Operation

In the Sensors Technology category, the use of RFI showed a modest decline this year, from 56 percent in 2004 to 43.9 percent, as depicted on Table 9. RFI continued to be the most used MO.

Table 9

FY05 Sensors Top Ten Methods of Operation

Rank	Method of Operation	Percent
1	Request for Information	43.88%
2	Exploitation of a foreign visit (CONUS)	3.60%
3	Exploitation of Relationships	4.32%
4	Acquisition of Controlled Technology	25.90%
5	Suspicious Internet Activity	5.76%
6	Cultural Commonality	0.72%
7	Targeting at Conventions/Expositions/Seminars	6.47%
8	Solicitation of Marketing Services	5.04%
9	Foreign Employees	0.72%
10	Other	3.60%

Acquisition of Controlled Technology indicated a significant increase, however, from 13.4 percent last year to 26 percent this year. Finally, Suspicious Internet Activity accounted for 5.8 percent of incidents, a three-fold increase over last year's 1.2 percent. Government entities accounted for 26.7 percent of incidents this year, or roughly the same as last year. Commercial entities' activity declined from 34.1 percent in 2004 to 21.9 percent.

E. ARMAMENTS & ENERGETIC MATERIALS TECHNOLOGY

Overview

Foreign targeting of Armaments and Energetic Materials Technology was largely unchanged from last year. Entities in Eurasia accounted for the greatest number of incidents in this category, supplanting the East Asia and Pacific region.

Government affiliated entities were identified in 32.4 percent of reports this year, up from 13.6 percent in 2004. This increase offset incidents involving foreign governments, which indicated a decrease from 40.9 percent to 22.9 percent this year. The most frequently used MO in this category was Acquisition of Controlled Technology, which increased to 29.5 percent of activity.

Examples of Armaments and Energetic Materials technology sought by foreign entities last year are: anti-tank guided missiles, air-to-air missiles, chemical propulsion technologies, explosives detection systems, fuzing technologies, anti-ship missiles, and vertical launch technologies.

Image 4: Sea Sparrow missile in flight

MCTL Vol. III Technology Categories

Table 10 shows the collection activity as reported by cleared U.S. defense contractors in 2005 for the Armaments and Energetic Materials Technology category. For an explanation of the technologies covered by each subcategory, please refer to the MCTL, Volume III.

Collection Activity by Region

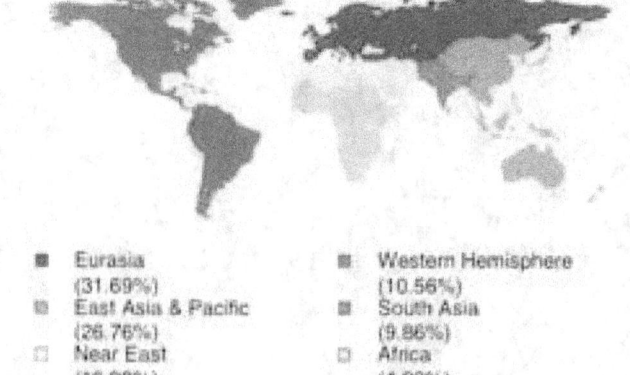

- ■ Eurasia (31.69%)
- ▨ East Asia & Pacific (26.76%)
- ☐ Near East (16.90%)
- ▨ Western Hemisphere (10.56%)
- ▨ South Asia (9.86%)
- ☐ Africa (4.23%)

Collection Attempts by Region

Eurasia supplanted the East Asia and Pacific region as the origin of most reported incidents in 2005. Eurasia accounted for 31.7 percent this year. East Asia and Pacific accounted for 26.8

Table 10

FY05 Armaments & Energetic Materials Technology Sub-Categories

Sub-Category	Percent
Small/Medium Caliber Weapon Systems	3.67%
Tactical Propulsion	5.50%
Safing, Arming, Fusing and Firing (SAFE)	3.67%
Guns, Artillery, and Other Launch Systems	4.59%
Guidance and Control	0.92%
Warhead Technologies	18.35%
Lethality and Vulnerability	0.92%
Energetic Materials	0.92%
Missile Systems	34.86%
Survivability, Armor, and Warhead Defeat Systems	9.17%
Armaments & Energetic Materials (Uncategorized)	17.43%

Table 11

FY05 Armaments Top Ten Methods of Operation

Rank	Method of Operation	Percent
1	Request for Information	24.66%
2	Exploitation of a foreign visit (CONUS)	7.53%
3	Exploitation of Relationships	8.22%
4	Acquisition of Controlled Technology	29.45%
5	Suspicious Internet Activity	6.16%
6	Cultural Commonality	2.74%
7	Targeting at Conventions/Expositions/Seminars	4.79%
8	Solicitation of Marketing Services	10.96%
9	Other	5.48%

percent of incidents involving Armaments and Energetic Materials. Incidents originating from the Western Hemisphere increased from 5.5 percent in 2004 to 10.6 percent this year. Africa also indicated an increase, from less than one percent to 4.2 percent. The Near East and South Asia regions accounted for fewer incidents than last year.

Methods of Operation

Acquisition of Controlled Technology was the most frequently used MO targeting Armaments and Energetic Materials. On Table 11, it accounted for 29.5 percent of incidents, a slight increase from 2004. RFI decreased from 32.6 percent last year to 24.7 percent in 2005. The percentage of entities directly affiliated with a foreign government changed significantly this year, decreasing from 40.9 percent to 22.9 percent. However, government affiliated entities were identified in 32.4 percent of incidents, a significant increase from last year's 13.6 percent. Other entities, commercial and individuals, changed little from last year.

F. ELECTRONICS TECHNOLOGY

Overview

Electronics Technology indicated a decline in activity, falling from fourth place last year to sixth in 2005. The Near East region had the most

Table 12

FY05 Electronics Technology Sub-Categories

Sub-Category	Percent
Electronics Components/Microwave Tubes	27.85%
Electronic Materials	3.80%
Electronic Fabrication	6.33%
Microelectronics	5.06%
Nanoelectronics	5.06%
Electronics (Uncategorized)	51.90%

activity in the category. Government affiliated entities indicated a significant increase from last year. Acquisition of Controlled Technology became the most employed MO in 2005. It was identified in 40 percent of reported incidents from cleared defense contractors.

Examples of Electronics Technology sought are: Field Programmable Gate Arrays (FPGA), microwave waveguide components, digital switching systems, Automated Test Equipment (ATE), planar array antennas, signal processing components, and electro-mechanical systems. Many of the technologies in the Electronics Technology category have legitimate dual-use applications.

MCTL Vol. III Technology Categories

Table 12 shows the collection activity as reported by cleared U.S. defense contractors in 2005 for the Electronics Technology category. For an explanation of the technologies covered by each subcategory, please refer to the MCTL, Volume III.

Collection Attempts by Region

Collection Activity by Region

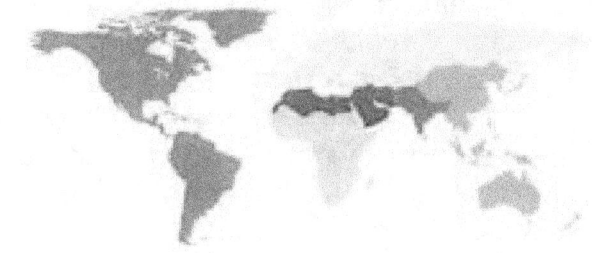

■ Near East (34.51%)	▨ South Asia (9.73%)
▨ East Asia & Pacific (27.43%)	▨ Western Hemisphere (7.08%)
☐ Eurasia (18.58%)	☐ Africa (2.65%)

Regional activity indicated a shift this year. The Near East had the most significant change, increasing from 22.4 percent of incidents in 2004 to 34.5 percent this year. Countries in the East Asia and Pacific region were second at 27.4 percent, a modest decrease from last year. Eurasia

13

also indicated a decline from 25.2 percent in 2004 to 18.6 percent this year. South Asia, the Western Hemisphere, and Africa also had fewer incidents. Each accounted for less than 10 percent of activity this year.

Methods of Operation

Table 13

FY05 Electronics Top Ten Methods of Operation

Rank	Method of Operation	Percent
1	Request for Information	21.82%
2	Exploitation of a foreign visit (CONUS)	5.45%
3	Exploitation of Relationships	6.36%
4	Acquisition of Controlled Technology	40.00%
5	Suspicious Internet Activity	6.36%
6	Targeting at Conventions/Expositions/Seminars	4.55%
7	Solicitation of Marketing Services	6.36%
8	Foreign Employees	3.64%
9	Other	4.55%
10	Unknown	0.91%

Acquisition of Controlled Technology indicated a significant increase, from 29.6 percent in 2004 to 40 percent of incidents in this category this year. RFI decreased to 21.8 percent as depicted on Table 13 from 50 percent last year. Events such as network vulnerability scans, incidents of hacking, and attempts to exploit known security vulnerabilities all comprise Suspicious Internet Activity. That MO indicated a slight increase this year, from 5.9 percent to 6.4 percent of activity related to Electronics Technology.
Government affiliated entities accounted for 39.5 percent of incidents in this category, a significant increase from last year's 15.3 percent.
Government entities were identified in 22.4 percent of incidents reported by cleared defense contractors for this category. Finally, commercial entities were traced to 19.7 percent of incidents.

G. SPACE SYSTEMS TECHNOLOGY

Overview

Space Systems moved from tenth position last year to seventh in 2005 in relative activity among technology categories. East Asia and Pacific was the origin of most identified activity related to Space Systems Technology. Government affiliated entities indicated a sharp increase in activity. Finally, Acquisition of Controlled Technology increased to nearly double last year's figure for the MO category.

Examples of Space Systems Technology targeted by foreign entities included: Radiation hardened electronics, ballistic missile simulation systems, space qualified optical systems, remote sensing systems, satellite command and control software, tracking and data relay satellite system, and satellite communications ground stations.

Table 14

FY05 Space Systems Technology Sub-Categories

Sub-Category	Percent
Electronics Components/ Microwave Tubes	27.85%
Electronic Materials	3.80%
Electronic Fabrication	6.33%
Microelectronics	5.06%
Nanoelectronics	5.06%
Electronics (Uncategorized)	51.90%

MCTL Vol. III Technology Categories

Table 14 shows the collection activity as reported by cleared U.S. defense contractors in 2005 for the Space Systems Technology category. For an explanation of the technologies covered by each subcategory, please refer to the MCTL, Volume III.

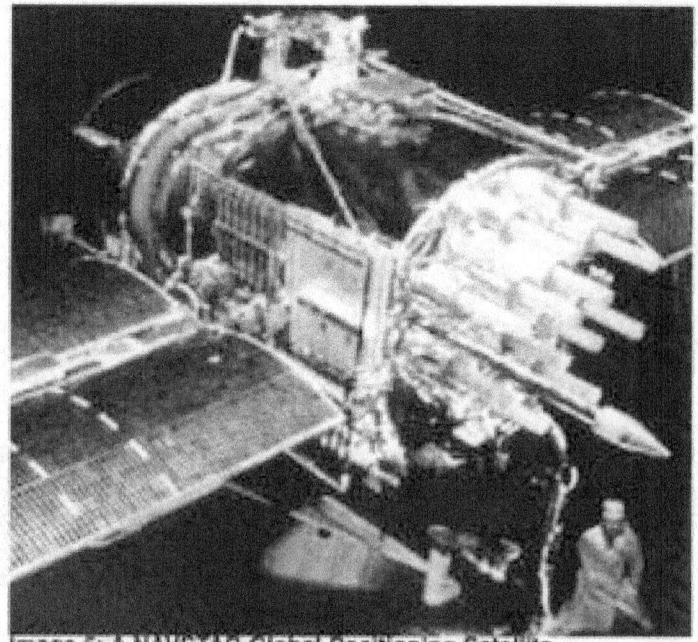

Image 5: A NAVSTAR Global Positioning Satellite

Collection Activity by Region

- ■ East Asia & Pacific (44.44%)
- ▨ South Asia (18.89%)
- ▢ Eurasia (14.44%)
- ▨ Near East (10.00%)
- ▨ Western Hemisphere (7.78%)
- ▢ Africa (4.44%)

Collection Attempts by Region

Countries in the East Asia and Pacific region were the most active in targeting restricted U.S. space systems and technologies for the second straight year. This region, at 44.4 percent of incidents this year, indicated a significant increase over last year's 30.3 percent. Africa also indicated increased activity, from no identified incidents last year to 4.4 percent of incidents in 2004. The other regions all indicated decreased activity.

Table 15

FY05 Space Systems Top Ten Methods of Operation

Rank	Method of Operation	Percent
1	Request for Information	29.35%
2	Exploitation of a foreign visit (CONUS)	6.52%
3	Exploitation of Relationships	4.35%
4	Acquisition of Controlled Technology	46.74%
5	Suspicious Internet Activity	1.09%
6	Cultural Commonality	1.09%
7	Targeting at Conventions/Expositions/Seminars	2.17%
8	Solicitation of Marketing Services	7.61%
9	Other	1.09%

Methods of Operation

On Table 15, reported attempts to acquire Space Systems Technology through direct purchases in 2005 nearly doubled to 46.7 percent of incidents in this category. Last year Acquisition of Controlled Technology as an MO amounted to 23.5 percent. Foreign RFI were less frequent, declining to 29.4 percent from last year's 50 percent of incidents. Government affiliated entities were identified in 32.9 percent of reports from cleared industry. This was a significant increase from last year's 12.9 percent. Foreign govern-

ments were involved in 26.3 percent of activity this year. Finally, commercial entities accounted for 19.7 percent in 2005, down from 38.7 percent in 2004.

H. MARINE SYSTEMS TECHNOLOGY

Overview

Marine Systems Technology did not make the DSS list of top ten technologies in 2004. This year, however, Marine Systems Technology amounted to 4.8 percent of incidents reported by cleared defense contractors.

More incidents were traced to Eurasia than other regions. RFI was the most employed MO, though Suspicious Internet Activity was also significant. Finally, government entities were most often identified in incidents involving Marine Systems Technology.

Examples of Marine Systems Technology sought are: Environmental systems, Littoral Combat Ship (LCS), maritime traffic control systems, anti-submarine warfare, advanced submarine technologies, aircraft carrier design and construction, and shipboard nuclear power systems.

Table 16

FY05 Marine Systems Technology Sub-Categories

Sub-Category	Percent
Propulsion	5.26%
Signature Control and Survivability	10.53%
Undersea Vehicles	42.11%
Advanced Hull Forms	3.51%
Marine Systems (Uncategorized)	38.60%

MCTL Vol. III Technology Categories

Table 16 shows the collection activity as reported by cleared U.S. defense contractors in 2005 for the Marine Systems Technology category. For an explanation of the technologies covered by each subcategory, please refer to the MCTL, Volume III.

Collection Attempts by Region

Countries of Eurasia were identified most often in reports from cleared industry, at 35.5 percent of

Image 6: SSN displaying TOMAHAWK missile tubes

Table 17

Rank	Method of Operation	Percent
1	Request for Information	29.17%
2	Exploitation of a foreign visit (CONUS)	11.11%
3	Exploitation of Relationships	2.78%
4	Acquisition of Controlled Technology	16.67%
5	Suspicious Internet Activity	25.00%
6	Cultural Commonality	1.39%
7	Solicitation of Marketing Services	9.72%
8	Potential Espionage Indicators	1.39%
9	Other	2.78%

FY05 Marine Systems Top Ten Methods of Operation

Activity at 25 percent. Acquisition of Controlled Technology was used in 16.7 percent of incidents.

I. MATERIALS & PROCESSING TECHNOLOGY

Overview

Despite an increase from last year, the Materials and Processing Technology category dropped one position to ninth place on the DSS list of top ten technologies. The East Asia and Pacific region, and the Near East, each appeared most often in reported activity. The percentage of incidents where government affiliated entities were identified indicated a dramatic increase this year. Acquisition of Controlled Technology was the most common MO in 2005.

Table 18

Sub-Category	Percent
Armor and Anti-Armor Materials	31.25%
Electrical Materials	2.06%
Structural Materials (High Strength and High Temperature)	8.33%
Special Function Materials	6.25%
Smart Materials and Structures	8.33%
Micromachined Materials and Structures [Including (MEMS)]	4.17%
Materials and Processing (Uncategorized)	39.58%

FY05 Materials & Processing Technology Sub-Categories

Examples of technology sought include: MEM technologies, composite armors, nano-fibers, magnetic smart materials, ballistic protective materials, bio-safety materials, and carbon-carbon materials.

activity in this category. The East Asia and Pacific region followed with 32.7 percent. The Near East accounted for 16.4 percent of inci-

Collection Activity by Region

- Eurasia (35.45%)
- East Asia & Pacific (32.73%)
- Near East (16.36%)
- Western Hemisphere (11.82%)
- South Asia (2.73%)
- Africa (0.91%)

dents, followed by the Western Hemisphere at 11.8 percent. South Asia and Africa had negligible activity in 2005.

Methods of Operation

Government entities, with 26.8 percent, were identified in most cases where it was possible to determine an affiliation. Commercial entities were identified in 19.6 percent of incidents. DSS was unable to identify the originating entity in 32.1 percent. As depicted on Table 17, RFI were used in 29.2 percent of incidents in this technology category, followed by Suspicious Internet

MCTL Vol. III Technology Categories

Table 18 shows the collection activity as reported by cleared U.S. defense contractors in 2005 for the Materials and Processing Technology category. For an explanation of the technologies covered by each subcategory, please refer to the MCTL, Volume III.

Collection Activity by Region

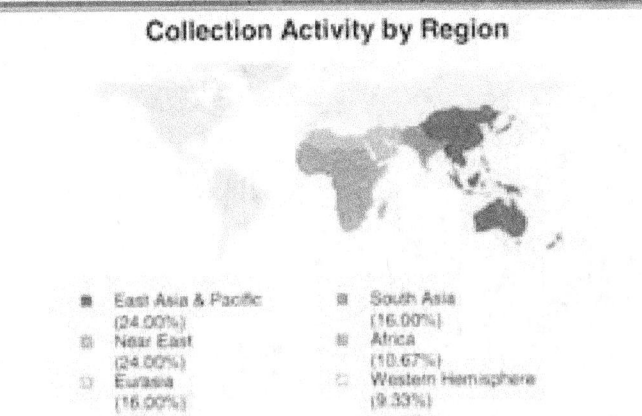

- East Asia & Pacific (24.00%)
- Near East (24.00%)
- Eurasia (16.00%)
- South Asia (16.00%)
- Africa (10.67%)
- Western Hemisphere (9.33%)

Collection Attempts by Region

Industry reports during 2005 indicated that East Asia and Pacific, and the Near East, were most active in this technology category. Each region accounted for 24 percent of incidents, increasing from last year. Eurasia and South Asia indicated decreased activity this year, accounting for 16 percent each. The percentage of incidents in this category that were traced to Africa increased from 5.3 percent in 2004 to 10.7 percent this year.

Table 19

Rank	FY05 Materials & Processing Top Ten Methods of Operation Method of Operation	Percent
1	Request for Information	34.48%
2	Exploitation of a foreign visit (CONUS)	3.45%
3	Acquisition of Controlled Technology	41.38%
4	Cultural Commonality	1.72%
5	Targeting at Conventions/Expositions/Seminars	3.45%
6	Solicitation of Marketing Services	13.79%
7	Foreign Employees	1.72%

Methods of Operation

Attempts to purchase Materials and Processing technology from cleared defense contractors occurred much more often this year, increasing from 15 percent of activity last year to 41.4 per-

cent this year. RFI declined to 34.5 percent from last year's 55 percent. The percentage of government affiliated entities identified in incidents related to this technology category increased significantly, from 7.9 percent in 2004 to 41.3 percent this year. Commercial entities were identified in 32.2 percent of incidents.

J. SIGNATURE CONTROL TECHNOLOGY

Overview

A modest decline in targeting of Signature Control Technology occurred in 2005. Cleared industry reports this year indicated significantly increased interest from South Asia. RFI and Acquisition of Controlled Technology were the most frequent MO. Government affiliated entities were identified most often.

Examples of targeted Signature Control Technology are: Radar cross-section modeling software, radar absorbing materials, signature reduction methodologies, anti-optical reflection coatings, anechoic materials, electromagnetic spectrum signatures, and optical camouflage systems.

MCTL Vol. III Technology Categories

Collection activity for the Signature Control Technology category was undefined as reported by cleared U.S. defense contractors in 2005. For an explanation of the technologies covered by each possible subcategory, please refer to the MCTL, Volume III.

Collection Activity by Region

- South Asia (33.33%)
- East Asia & Pacific (27.27%)
- Near East (19.70%)
- Eurasia (12.12%)
- Western Hemisphere (7.58%)
- Africa (0.00%)

Collection Attempts by Region

An apparent surge in interest among South Asian countries in Signature Control Technology increased their presence in cleared contractor reports from 12.5 percent in 2004 to 33.3 percent this year. Countries in the East Asia and Pacific region indicated a slight decrease in activity, from 28.8 percent to 27.3 percent this year. The Near East increased slightly to 19.7 percent of incidents in this technology category. Eurasia indicated a significant decline in activity, from 28.8 percent last year to 12.1 percent in 2005. Africa and the Western Hemisphere were identified in slightly fewer incidents this year.

Image 7: A B-2 bomber during refueling

Table 20

FY05 Signature Control **Top Ten Methods of Operation**

Rank	Method of Operation	Percent
1	Request for Information	47.46%
2	Exploitation of a foreign visit (CONUS)	1.69%
3	Exploitation of Relationships	1.69%
4	Acquisition of Controlled Technology	47.46%
5	Solicitation of Marketing Services	1.69%

Methods of Operation

On Table 20, RFI and actual attempts to acquire controlled technology accounted for 47.5 percent of incidents in this technology category. These were the most employed MOs. Employment of other MOs occurred in very few incidents. Government affiliated entities were identified in 58.5 percent of reports from cleared defense industry, a significant increase from last year's 18.4 percent. Commercial entities were identified in far fewer reports, declining from 44.7 percent in 2004 to 13.2 percent this year.

V. FUTURE TRENDS ASSESSMENT

DSS foresees a continuing trend of increased suspicious contact reports from cleared defense contractors. The globalization of defense business will increase the threat from strategic competitors who will use legitimate business activities as a venue to illegally transfer U.S. technology. The number of countries identified in reports, on a steady increase over the past five years, likely will level off. However, the use of third countries to disguise targeting by major foreign governments/competitors will ensure that the number of countries in SCRs remains high.

Information Systems Technology, due to its potential for enhancing the efficiency of command, control, communications, and intelligence, will continue to be a priority technology target for many countries. The steady increase in incidents over the past two years where foreign entities target modeling and simulation technology is also noteworthy. It may be a reflection of the number of weapons development programs in many countries as they attempt to emulate U.S. military advances. The recent shift in collector affiliations from commercial to government affiliated and government entities may also be related to the relatively early stages of these weapons development programs. The increase in incidents of attempted direct purchases of controlled items appears to be a corollary development, consistent with the increase in government and government affiliated efforts.

The apparent across-the-board surge in activity from East Asia and Pacific countries will continue in the short term as gaps in technological capability become apparent in their weapons development processes. Lasers and Optics Technology and Aeronautics appear to be priority technology targets for this region. Materials and Processing will continue to experience strong foreign interest, since some countries in the East Asia and Pacific region have designated this area as a leading industry for future economic growth.

DSS also anticipates an increase in suspicious Internet activity against cleared defense contractors. The potential gain from even one successful computer intrusion makes it an attractive, relatively low-risk, option for any country seeking access to sensitive information stored on U.S. computer networks. The risk to sensitive information on U.S. computer systems will increase as more countries develop capabilities to exploit those systems.

These developments, particularly increased commercial endeavors with foreign entities, complicate the security and counterintelligence community's ability to distinguish between legitimate business and activities designed to facilitate illegitimate acquisition of U.S. technology. Foreign entities will likely use ostensibly legitimate business to target and exploit U.S. firms that develop sensitive technologies. Many countries already deem it to be in their national interest to acquire any and all U.S. military and dual-use technology, no matter how insignificant, in order to assemble a body of technological work for domestic industries to exploit. The threat environment is multidimensional: Countering that threat requires innovative thinking on the part of U.S. defense security professionals.

VI. HIGHLIGHTS OF SUSPICIOUS CONTACT REPORTS

Information Systems Technology

A foreign entity emailed a cleared defense contractor with a request for a price quote on 11 different export controlled items used in electronic and communications intelligence gathering. That cleared defense contractor has reported six incidents of foreign interest in such export controlled products.

Lasers & Optics Technology

A foreign firm sent an unsolicited email request for a price quote for export controlled dual-use laser technology from a cleared defense contractor. The firm claimed that the ND:YAG laser with aiming beam was for a biomedical physics project. This item can be used in both commercial and military applications. Military uses include range finders and target designators. The laser is on the U.S. Department of Commerce's Commerce Control List, which identifies items which require validated export licenses for shipment to all or specified countries.

Aeronautics Technology

A U.S. cleared defense contractor has been involved in an unclassified contract with a firm in East Asia to provide software and hardware interfaces for a UAV ground control system, which was previously purchased from the cleared defense contractor. A general manager at the East Asian firm requested a visit to the U.S. contractor's facility to follow up some warranty repairs for the UAV ground system. Shortly after the request, the East Asian firm informed the U.S. contractor that it intended to send two representatives to observe the repair of the equipment. The U.S. contractor had several subsequent contacts with the firm's management in an attempt to persuade them that the visit was unnecessary and would slow down the repair process due to the security problems that their on-site presence would cause. Although the U.S. contractor thought they had convinced the foreign firm not to send any representatives, within a week two engineers from the foreign firm arrived at the U.S. contractor's classified facility. The U.S. contractor refused to allow them access to the classified facility and provided updates to the repair process at their hotel. Both engineers returned to their country without visiting the U.S. facility.

This aggressive effort to visit the U.S. contractor's facility may have been a veiled attempt to collect information on other high-interest UAV programs at the facility. This was the fourth suspicious contact report that DSS has recorded regarding the East Asian firm's interest in the U.S. contractor's UAV platforms and supporting equipment since 2003. This foreign firm's aggressive collection efforts against the U.S. contractor's UAV technology has occurred in both the United States and in the East Asian nation, and has targeted non-releasable items including UAV datalinks, take off and landing system technology, communication links, stem design and simulation technology, remote video terminal and portable control systems

Sensors Technology

An employee of a Near East defense firm, while working on a joint contract with a U.S. defense contractor, was able to place one of his firm's computers on the U.S. contractor's classified and controlled test network. Ostensibly, this was to control the test of an expendable torpedo decoy designed by the Near East firm. However, the test network was also used for testing a U.S. designed, classified and export-controlled second generation torpedo defense suite.

At the conclusion of the test cycle, a U.S. employee requested that the foreign classified disk and hard drive be placed under control of the facility security officer. The Near East firm's employee refused the request, stating that the U.S. firm was not cleared for his country's classified information.

Within months of the employee departing the U.S. firm with his classified disk and hard drive, the Near East firm announced its second generation torpedo defense suite with similar characteristics and capabilities as the cleared defense contractor's system. This incident underscores the inherent risks in joint ventures, where foreign collectors have opportunities to exploit the relationship.

VII. Appendix 1: Methods of Operation (MO) Definitions, Indicators, and Countermeasures

Request for Information. A Request for Information (RFI) is an unsolicited inquiry from a known or unknown source concerning classified, sensitive, or export-controlled information. There are two types of RFI: direct and indirect. A direct RFI occurs when a suspicious entity specifically targets website advertisements. One example of an unwanted, but indirect RFI, occurs when a trade journal reviews a cleared defense contractor's product or technology. After the publicity, the cleared defense contractor often receives numerous suspicious, but "solicited," reader service inquiries from embargoed nations.

Acquisition of Technology. This MO involves foreign attempts to gain access to

Requests for Information (RFI)	
Indicators	Countermeasure
• Technology is ITAR controlled • Cleared defense contractor does not normally conduct business with the foreign requester • Request originates from an embargoed nation or represents unidentified third party • Request is unsolicited or unwarranted • Requester claims to represent an official government agency but avoids proper channels to make the request • Initial request targets an employee who does not know the sender and is not in the sales or marketing department • Requester is fishing for information or asking for highly technical information in a field in which she is not conversant • Requester is located in a country known to target the U.S. cleared defense industry	• Educate employees about the threat • On company websites, include a notice that products and technologies are export controlled to screen out requests from foreign entities • Ask who the requester represents and why they seek the requested information • Incorporate security into web design and advertising and initiate an active monitoring solution website • Report the contact to the Facility Security Officer, Industrial Security Representative, and DSS CI Office because other cleared defense contractor facilities may have also been targeted for similar technologies

an individual or organization. An indirect RFI occurs when a suspicious entity solicits information by using technical journals and sensitive technologies by purchasing U.S technology. In some cases, a foreign entity may attempt to acquire the company that develops the sensitive technology.

Acquisition of Technology	
Indicators	Countermeasure
• Foreign individuals or competitors seek a position in the U.S. company that affords access to restricted technology • Statements that licenses are unnecessary • Foreign company requests a U.S. company send information/products to another U.S. based company for foreign transfer or via email to foreign addresses • Requester appears to be skirting controls • Multiple similar requests made over time • Foreign competitors purchase U.S. defense firms	• Perform due diligence on the buyer and the end user • Ask about the end use of the solicited technology or information • Scrutinize employees hired at the request of a foreign entity/business partner • Request a threat assessment from the Industrial Security Representative or DSS CI Office

Solicitation and Marketing of Services	
Indicators	Countermeasure
• Offers to provide offshore software support for defense-related projects • Invitations for cultural exchanges, individual-to-individual exchanges, or ambassador programs • Offers to act as a sales or purchasing agent in foreign countries • Internships sponsored by a foreign government or foreign business	• Implement a technology control plan • Request a threat assessment from the Industrial Security Representative or DSS CI Office • Scrutinize employees hired at the request of a foreign entity or business partner • Report the contact to the Facility Security Officer, Industrial Security Representative, and DSS CI Office because other cleared defense contractor facilities may have been offered similar services • Be wary of cultural exchanges

Reporting indicates the majority of acquisition attempts are directed at purchasing specific components or technologies.

Solicitation of Marketing Services. In this instance, foreign individuals with technical backgrounds offer services to research facilities, academic institutions, and cleared defense contractors. Several incidents have involved foreign nationals seeking postdoctoral fellowships at cleared universities or employment at companies involved in cutting-edge technologies.

Exploitation of Foreign Visit. A foreign visitor includes one-time visitors, long-term visitors (exchange employees, official government representatives, students) and frequent visitors (foreign sales representatives). A suspicious contact can occur before, during, and after a visit. The primary factor contributing to suspicious foreign visits is based upon the extent to which the foreign visitor requests access to

Exploitation of Foreign Visit	
Indicators	Countermeasure
• Foreign Liaison Officer or embassy official attempts to conceal official identity during commercial visits • Suspected hidden agendas versus the original purpose of the visit • Last minute and unannounced persons are added to the visiting party • Presence of wandering visitors who act offended when confronted • Foreign entity attempts a commercial visit or uses a U.S. based third party to arrange a visit after the original foreign visit request is denied • Visitors ask questions outside the scope of the approved visit to receive a courteous or spontaneous answer • Visitors claim business-related interest but lack experience researching and developing technology • Visitors ask to meet personnel from their own countries and attempt to establish continuing contact with them	• Educate all cleared defense contractor employees involved with the foreign visit about the threat • Request a country threat assessment from the Industrial Security Representative or DSS CI Office • Ensure personnel (escorts and meeting attendees) understand the scope of the visit and topics not open for discussion • Provide a sufficient number of escorts for the foreign visitors to limit movements and monitor foreign visitor conduct • Conduct frequent checks during foreign visits to determine if the foreign interests are attempting to circumvent security agreements • Be aware of gang tackling, when multiple individuals attempt to overwhelm one individual with questions • Do not introduce visitors to personnel from their own countries; only use such personnel where it makes business sense (i.e. for translation or because she is a recognized expert)

cleared defense contractor facilities or discusses information outside the scope of the approved visit. It is important to recognize long-term visitors often establish personal relationships with cleared defense contractor employees in order to elicit information and may do so only gradually or after a friendship has been established. More importantly, even discussions of export-controlled technologies require an export license.

Targeting at Conventions. Foreign entities target conventions, seminars, and exhibits because these functions provide access to cleared defense contractors, new technologies, and subject matter experts. Consequently, the foreign entities will utilize

multiple MOs to solicit classified, sensitive, and export-restricted information. These events also afford a unique opportunity to study, compare, and photograph U.S. technology at one location.

Foreign-hosted conventions, seminars, and exhibits are more vulnerable to exploitation. Foreign intelligence services (FIS) employ technical collection (electronic surveillance) and execute "entrapment" ploys such as placing the targeted individual in a compromising situation. It is interesting to note that foreign scientists and foreign technical experts often pose a greater technology collection risk than foreign intelligence officers. This is because international seminars are normally comprised of leading sci-

Targeting at Exhibits, Conventions, and Seminars	
Indicators	Countermeasure
• Conversations involve classified, sensitive, or export-controlled technologies or products • The foreign country or organization hosting the event unsuccessfully attempted to visit facilities in the past • Receive an all expenses paid invitation to lecture in a foreign nation • Entities want a summary of the requested presentation or brief 6-12 months prior to the lecture date • Excessive or suspicious photography and filming of technology and products • Foreign attendees wear false name tags • Casual conversations during and after the event hinting at future contacts or relations • Foreign attendees business cards do not match stated affiliations	• Implement a technology control plan for products and proprietary information taken to foreign countries • Monitor any follow-up requests for information because they are often collection attempts • Report suspicious contacts to the Facility Security Officer, Industrial Security Representative, and DSS CI Office • Determine what type of information is potentially susceptible to exploitation (who, what, where, when, why) • Brief convention attendees about the threat and discuss methods of mitigating elicitation techniques • Display mock-up products instead of real equipment • Request a convention and country threat assessment from the Industrial Security Representative or DSS CI Office • Restrict revealing information to what is only necessary for arranging travel accommodations • Determine if equipment or software can be adequately protected • Beware of gang tackling: if two or more people ask simultaneous questions, do not speak without thinking; get two colleagues to help you or tell one person you will get back to him

entists and foreign technical experts who tailor questions on specific technical areas pertinent to their own work. Past Suspicious Contact Reports (SCR) also reveal overt and subtle methods of soliciting information. For example, one technique known as "gang tackling" occurs when multiple individuals approach an individual with general questions. The individual becomes overwhelmed with the number of questions and when one collector strategically asks the "real" question, the individual accidentally reveals the answer. Additionally, foreign entities will surreptitiously target cleared defense contractor employees by sitting next to them and casually initiating conversations. This initial contact establishes a point of reference and relationship that may lead to exploitation at

business or academic relationships often place foreign entities alongside U.S. personnel and technology, thus facilitating access to protected programs. One growing security concern is the increased use of foreign research facilities and software development companies based overseas for commercial projects related to protected programs. Technology is more susceptible to foreign exploitation when a company relinquishes direct control of its processes or products to another company. Moreover, outsourcing to foreign firms often place foreign workers in close proximity to protected programs. Though high technology programs received the greatest public attention, low technology programs such as fabrics for the military Battle Dress Uniform (BDU), are equally susceptible to foreign exploitation.

Exploitation: Relationships	
Indicators	Countermeasure
• Foreign representatives mail or fax documents written in a foreign language to a foreign embassy or foreign country • Foreign entities repeatedly request access to the LAN, want unrestricted facility access, and target company personnel for information • Foreign entities request detailed technical data during bidding process and then cancel the contract • Potential technology-sharing agreements during the joint venture favors foreign entity • Foreign organization provides more foreign representatives than is necessary for the project • New employees hired from the foreign parent company or its foreign partners ask to access classified or export-controlled data	• Implement a technology control plan for products and proprietary information taken to foreign countries or have a detailed Standard Practice and Procedures • Review and translate foreign language correspondence • Provide foreign representatives with stand-alone computers • Share minimum amount of information appropriate to the scope of the joint venture/research • Train employees on the scope of the project and how to deal with and report elicitation attempts • Refuse to accept unnecessary foreign representatives into the facility

a later date. Finally, cleared defense contractors must recognize FIS officers will likely debrief their own scientists and employees who attended these conventions, seminars, and exhibits.

Exploitation of Joint Venture/Research Relationships. Joint Ventures and R&D partnerships provide significant collection opportunities for foreign interests. These

Suspicious Internet Activity. The explosive growth of the Internet and abundance of free email accounts has resulted in increased cases involving Suspicious Internet Activity. Internet hacking is included in this technique because the majority of hacking attempts are correlated with probing efforts to exploit computer network weaknesses for future exploitation. One

Suspicious Internet Activity	
Indicators	Countermeasure
• Computer probes and emails with attachments known to carry viruses and other computer exploits • Network attacks originate from foreign IP address or ISPs • Attacks last more than a day • Multiple intrusion attempts are used with multiple passwords and scripts	• Use a firewall monitoring software that logs intrusion attempts and malicious activity • Have appropriate level of protection in place to repel such an attack • When a probe is noted, increase network security alert status

reported Internet probe targeted a defense contractor's unclassified network and lasted over 24 hours. Though the original source of the attack was likely masked, the probes were traced to IP addresses allocated to a "girl's school" in an East Asian country. The suspicious entity very likely concealed the true identity in order to deter network security administrators. Probing a network system is not a crime, but once a port is breached by an unauthorized entity it becomes a crime.

Targeting of U.S. Personnel Abroad.
This MO involves targeting U.S. defense contractor employees traveling overseas. Targeting can occur at airports and past techniques include luggage searches,

Targeting of U.S. Personnel Abroad	
Indicators	Countermeasure
• Suspicious or unknown individuals ask specific questions regarding private and professional subjects • Defense employee observes any activity indicating possible surveillance • Hotel room and personal items appear to have been searched or accessed • Foreign officials confiscate computers or media • Employees repeatedly identified for official questioning • Employee is assigned to the same general hotel area (room or floor) during multiple visits • Hotel provides copiers, shredders, computers and other business equipment • Business equipment (computers, cell phones, PDAs) are "lost" or confiscated	• Complete a pre-travel security briefing and do not publicize travel plans • Maintain control of all sensitive items • Lock hotel room doors and remember room arrangement prior to departure • Limit sensitive discussions • Avoid using computers or fax equipment at foreign hotels or business centers for sensitive matters • Ignore or deflect intrusive or suspicious conversations and questions regarding personal and professional information • Retain unwanted (no longer needed) sensitive material until it can be securely disposed of • Do not use unsecured copiers or shredders for classified or sensitive documents • Do not bring classified or sensitive materials unless necessary and specifically authorized to do so • When traveling, remove hard drives, floppies, and CDs from computers to carry separately, so they won't be "lost" or confiscated

unauthorized use of laptop computers, and extensive questioning beyond normal security measures. Other travelers have received excessively "helpful" service by host government representatives and hotel staff. It is important to recognize copiers and shredders can contain built-in scanners to copy the data. Industry reporting also indicates foreign entities use traditional FIS collection methods such as placing listening devices in rooms, searching hotel rooms, inspecting electronic equipment, and positioning people to eavesdrop on conversations.

VIII. Appendix 2: Recent Cases

Following a failed hacking attempt by a foreign IP on a contractor's web page, the contractor's computer audit revealed the same foreign IP address had conducted an identical attack across the entire network. It is assumed that the contractor's five subsidiary networks were infiltrated.

A U.S. resident foreign national, recently indicted on espionage charges, was linked to a series of hacking attempts that occurred at facilities he visited. A week prior to his delegation's visit to a cleared defense contractor, the suspect began to log hacking attempts from his country of origin. The attacks stopped upon completion of his visit.

A female foreign national seduced an American male translator to give her his password in order to log on to his unclassified network. Upon discovery of this security breach, a computer audit revealed foreign intelligence service viruses throughout the system.

A cleared defense contractor's employee was observed recording classified briefings using a voice-recording pen. When confronted by security officials, she denied having such a device. A search of her belongings uncovered the recorder. She changed her story, stating that her boss had approved the use of the recorder because of her medical condition (carpal tunnel syndrome). Her boss denied knowledge.

A film processing company contacted the FBI after it developed film from a cleared contractor that contained classified images of satellites and their blueprints. From the photos it was determined that the pictures were taken from an adjacent office's window.

On at least three separate occasions between October 2005 and January 2006, cleared defense contractors' employees traveling through Canada have discovered radio frequency transmitters embedded in Canadian coins placed on their persons.

A mid-level manager working for a cleared defense contractor developing the Army Future Combat System was caught misusing sensitive test equipment she was not authorized to use. She purposefully missed a DSS interview about the incident, and then made sure her subordinate was away on business when DSS came to interview him. Subsequent to her termination, she attempted to remove a classified hard drive from the facility

2006 Technology Collection Trends in the U.S. Defense Industry
Feedback Form

DSSCI welcomes feedback from the U.S. cleared defense industry. Please provide your comments and feedback below and notify your DSS Field Office or mail this form to DSSCI, 1340 Braddock Place, Alexandria, VA 22314.

Cleared Defense Contractor Name: _____

CAGE Code: _____

Point of Contact: _____

Address: _____

Email/Phone: _____

Issue: _____
_____
_____
_____
_____
_____
_____
_____

Discussion: _____
_____
_____
_____
_____
_____
_____
_____
_____
_____
_____

Recommendation: _____
_____
_____
_____
_____
_____
_____

www.ingramcontent.com/pod-product-compliance
Lightning Source LLC
Chambersburg PA
CBHW080747290526
45790CB00008B/3364